YORK NOTES
KEY STAGE 3

Macbeth

William Shakespeare

Notes by James Sale

Longman   York Press

York Press
322 Old Brompton Road, London SW5 9JH

Pearson Education Limited
Edinburgh Gate, Harlow, Essex CM20 2JE, United Kingdom
Associated companies, branches and representatives throughout
the world

First published 2000

ISBN 0-582-43146-8

Illustrated by Gerry Grace
Designed by Vicki Pacey
Phototypeset by Gem Graphics, Trenance, Mawgan Porth, Cornwall
Printed in Great Britain by Henry Ling Limited, Dorchester, Dorset

Contents

Preface   **4**

Introduction   **5**
     How to study a Shakespeare play   **5**
     Shakespeare's life   **7**
     Background to the play   **8**

Summaries   **10**
     Illustrated summary   **10**
     Detailed summaries & tests   **12**
       Act I   **12**   Key Scene Act I scenes 6 and 7
       Act II   **21**
       Act III   **29**
       Act IV   **37**
       Act V   **43**

Commentary   **51**
     Themes   **51**
     Characters   **52**
     Shakespeare's Language   **57**

Key Stage 3 & Shakespeare   **59**
     Examinations   **59**
     Success at Key Stage 3   **61**

Literary terms   **66**

Key Scene Act IV scene 1

Preface

York Notes Key Stage 3 guides are designed to give you the help you need to tackle the plays of Shakespeare, a requirement for the National Tests.

The English tests (sometimes called SATs) are taken in the final term of Year 9. Pupils must sit two papers: Paper 1 on Reading and Writing and Paper 2 on Key Scenes taken from a Shakespeare play chosen by your teacher. The papers are marked by external examiners and the results are published at the end of July, in the form of a Level for English.

This symbol shows the Key Scenes which will feature in your 2000 National Test

Each of these Notes will provide a biography of Shakespeare and close examination of one of the set plays, and include a summary of each scene in the play as well as detailed summaries of the Key Scenes on which the National Test focuses. To check your progress, tests are included on each Act. Commentary is also provided on themes, characters and language.

York Notes Key Stage 3 are written by English teachers and examiners with an expert knowledge of the subject. They show you how to succeed in your Key Stage 3 tests, taking you through the play and offering practical guidance.

York Notes Key Stage 3 guides are ideal for

* Understanding Shakespeare
* Preparing for exams
* Improving your Level

The author of this Note is James Sale. He is an experienced teacher and has been head of drama, head of English and deputy headmaster. He has been involved with many educational books on poetry and drama.

The text used in these Notes is the New Penguin Shakespeare series, 1995.

Introduction

How to study a Shakespeare play

The National Curriculum in English makes it compulsory for Key Stage 3 students to study for an examination on a Shakespeare play. This book aims to guide you through this task by explaining carefully the development of the story of your chosen play, and by setting out the important features which you will need to include in your examination response.

Shakespeare wrote his plays for performance on a stage. The best way in to this play is of course to go to a theatre and see it live. If you are unable to do this, then hire it on a video or listen to it on audiotape or CD.

One of the chief reasons for the greatness of these plays is that they are entertaining. They are studied in class because their true quality may not be revealed in a single visit to the theatre.

Use the points given below as a check-list to help you to a fuller understanding of what the play is about:

* Follow the story-line – who are the winners and losers? Does the story end in the way you would have chosen? Or would you change its ending? Why?
* Look at the characters – which ones do you like and which ones do you dislike? Are you happy with what happens to them at the end of the play?
* Look at the staging of the play – is the set what you would have expected? If not, why not? Do you think that you might have been mistaken in your view of what the set should have been? Why?
* Look at the costumes – are they what you would have expected? Again, if not, why not? Do the characters' costumes tell you anything about the characters themselves?

* Think of the special effects, like lighting and sound – what did they add to your enjoyment of the production?

Remember each generation interprets Shakespeare in a way that makes sense to its audiences. If you see Shakespeare's plays as museum pieces, you are unlikely to be very entertained by them.

Think about this: the best students are those who identify with the plays they watch. What do you think this play can tell you about life in the new millennium?

Find answers to that question and you will truly have made a success of your first experience with Shakespeare study.

Shakespeare's life

Family life

William Shakespeare was born at Stratford-upon-Avon in 1564. There is a record of his christening on 26 April, so we can assume he was born shortly before that date. His father, John Shakespeare, was a glove-maker and trader who later became high bailiff of Stratford; his mother, Mary Arden, was the daughter of a landowner.

In 1582 Shakespeare married Anne Hathaway, a woman eight years older than himself. Their first child, Susanna, was christened in May 1583, and in 1585 twins Hamnet and Judith were born.

Writing

Sometime after 1585 Shakespeare left Stratford and went to London where he became an actor and a dramatist. He worked first with a group of actors called Lord Pembroke's Men and later with a company called the Lord Chamberlain's Men (later the King's Men). His earliest plays were performed around 1590 to 1594. He was successful in the theatre from the start.

The last years

Although Shakespeare lived and worked for most of his life in London, he obviously did not forget Stratford, and in about 1610 he returned to live there permanently.

Shakespeare wrote a will in January 1616, leaving money to people he knew in Stratford and to some of his actor-friends. He died on 23 April 1616.

Background to the play

Many writers throughout history have composed their works for kings, queens or rich or important people; this is called patronage

Macbeth was written sometime between 1603 and 1606. This coincides with the accession of James VI of Scotland to the English throne, as James I of England, in 1603. The play was certainly written with James in mind.

Firstly, it caters for the interests and expertise of James: its fascination with the supernatural would attract his attention. Witchcraft, apparitions and ghosts, and the King's Evil were areas of great concern to James.

Secondly, it compliments James by making his ancestor, Banquo, a hero in the play.

Thirdly, the play explores the issue of kingship and loyalty. These were of profound importance to James, who had survived an assassination attempt early in life.

Fourthly, the play is intimately related to the topical events of the Gunpowder Plot of 1605 and the subsequent trials of its conspirators. This failed coup was sensational in a number of ways – the sheer audacity of trying to blow up Parliament amazed the country, as did the scale of the treachery involved. Treason is related to the wider theme of appearances. For example Lady Macbeth advises Macbeth to 'look like the innocent flower, / But be the serpent under't' (I.5.63–4).

Three witches greet Macbeth with Banquo. They proclaim 'Macbeth, that shalt be king hereafter!'

Macbeth sees a ghost of Banquo at the banquet.

Macbeth kills Duncan, with Lady Macbeth taking the bloodstained dagger back to the room.

Summaries

Act I

Scene 1
We meet the witches

In the middle of a storm three witches, sometimes called the Weird Sisters, appear. Their riddling rhymes indicate that they intend to meet Macbeth.

Comment

The witches are highly ambiguous creatures – whether they are human is debatable. They create a sense of mystery: they will meet when 'the battle's lost and won' (line 4), which seems a contradiction.

The fact that they are evil is shown in their final **couplet** (see Literary Terms). According to them, 'Fair is foul, and foul is fair' (line 9): good is bad and bad is good. The witches are overturning God's natural order.

Scene 2
Macbeth and Banquo's bravery

King Duncan and his court receive news from a wounded captain that the battle against the traitor and rebel Macdonwald and his army was evenly balanced until Macbeth and Banquo destroyed him and his troops. But as this occurs, reinforcements from the King of Norway and the traitor, the Thane of Cawdor, counterattack Macbeth and Banquo. However, these two are not at all dismayed; but as the captain is taken away to tend his wounds, the outcome is still unsure. The Thane of Ross arrives to report that, through the fighting spirit of Macbeth, Duncan's army has won a great victory. Duncan declares that the traitor Thane of Cawdor is to be executed and Macbeth is to receive his title and estates as a reward.

| Comment

From the shadowy world of the witches we switch to the immediate and physical world of battle and action.

Notice that we have not yet met Macbeth. The witches mentioned him earlier. Now the Captain and Ross do. The battle is primitive and bloody, but their descriptions emphasise a heroic quality about the proceedings, and Macbeth's part in them. Duncan himself generously praises Macbeth, and the final adjective he uses about him is 'noble' (line 70).

The use of **dramatic irony** (see Literary Terms) is particularly important as this play explores the differences between what appears to be so and what actually is. Duncan comments that the Thane of Cawdor shall no more deceive him. He does not know, as we do, that when Macbeth becomes Thane of Cawdor he will also be a traitor. Ironically, it is in becoming the Thane of Cawdor that Macbeth's ambition to become king grows.

| Scene 3

The witches tell Macbeth and Banquo of the future

The storm still blows on the three witches as they boast of their exploits. They cast a spell as they prepare to meet Macbeth. He arrives with Banquo and both are shocked by the appearance of the witches, who greet Macbeth and inform him that he will become Thane of

Cawdor and also King of Scotland. Macbeth is stunned by these prophecies, and Banquo demands they inform him of his future. He is told that although he will not be king, his offspring will be. Macbeth insists that the witches explain how they know these things, since they are frankly incredible. But the witches vanish as abruptly as they came.

Macbeth becomes Thane of Cawdor

Macbeth and Banquo briefly discuss the 'insane' prophecies they have just heard, and at that point Ross and Angus arrive to bring thanks from King Duncan. Ross tells Macbeth he has become the Thane of Cawdor. Macbeth and Banquo are both amazed, and we begin to see Macbeth's ambition expressed in the asides – or **soliloquys** (see Literary Terms) – he delivers to the audience. Banquo warns of the danger of trusting such supernatural messages, but Macbeth is lost in his own thoughts, thinking through all the implications. Eventually, he is stirred and agrees to ride towards the king. In private to Banquo, he suggests they speak about the revelations at some future point, which Banquo agrees to.

Comment

The witches' boasting invokes evil but also reveals some limitations to their powers. They may have the power to change shape, but the rat has no tail (line 9) – in other words, is unnaturally and imperfectly formed. Furthermore, in their attack upon the 'master o' the *Tiger*' (line 7) they admit 'his bark cannot be lost' (line 24). What they do to him, however, is reminiscent of Macbeth's future condition: 'dry as hay' (line 18), sleepless (lines 19–20), and he will 'dwindle, peak, and pine' (line 23).

Macbeth's first words – 'So foul and fair a day I have not seen' (line 37) – echo the witches' words 'Fair is foul, and foul is fair' (I.1.9). This suggests he is already in tune with their way of thinking.

Banquo's description of the witches is important in seeing how unnatural they are: they seem to be women but are not. Banquo thinks they are evil: 'What! Can the devil speak true?' (line 105). Macbeth disagrees.

Note how keen Macbeth is to hear more of this 'strange intelligence' (line 74): 'Would they had stayed!' (line 81). Their words are exactly what he wants to hear and this can only be because they touch a nerve already present in Macbeth.

Banquo's warning to Macbeth concerning the 'instruments of darkness' (line 123) might also be seen as prophetic – Macbeth is betrayed as a result of believing these 'truths', and he comes to realise this in his final confrontation with Macduff (V.6.58–61).

The **soliloquy** (see Literary Terms) beginning 'Two truths are told' (line 126) shows that Macbeth all too quickly, after becoming Thane of Cawdor, begins that process of imagining the steps he will need to take – that is, murdering Duncan – to become king. At this point the real horror of doing the deed seems to be balanced by a morbid fascination at the thought of it.

Scene 4

King Duncan names Malcolm, his son, as his heir

King Duncan asks his son, Malcolm, about the execution of the Thane of Cawdor. He is told that Cawdor died repenting of his actions and with dignity. Macbeth and Banquo arrive and are thanked by Duncan for their efforts. Duncan announces that his son, Malcolm, is to be his heir and also that he will visit Macbeth in his castle at Inverness. Macbeth leaves to prepare for the arrival of the King, but we learn that the announcement of Malcolm as heir is a bitter blow to him. If Macbeth is to be king, then this is something he must overcome. In his absence, Duncan praises Macbeth to Banquo.

Scene 5

Lady Macbeth is determined to become queen

Lady Macbeth reads a letter from her husband informing her of his success in battle and, more importantly, of his encounter with the witches. He believes their words, and is excited about his eventual destiny to be king – and for her to be queen. She is worried that Macbeth is too soft a person to be able to take the crown. She vows that she will assist him through the 'valour of my tongue' (line 25). On hearing – to her great surprise and then delight – that the King himself will be staying in their castle overnight, she calls on demonic spirits to strengthen her determination and to destroy any weakness of pity. Macbeth enters and she immediately sets to work persuading him. He says little but she insists that the deed must be done, that she will personally organise its operation, and finally that failure to kill Duncan would be a form of fear.

Comment

Lady Macbeth immediately understands the full implications of her husband's letter and her response is uncompromising: her husband must be what he has been promised. She has no misgivings and she overwhelms her husband when he appears. She instantly taps into the spirit world: her spirits will invade Macbeth's ear, and she invokes spirits to possess her body. The point about her 'unsex'-ing and her 'woman's breasts' no longer being used for milk but murder, mirrors the ambiguous sexuality of the witches themselves. It is as if, at this level of evil, one abandons being either male or female – one is a neutral 'it'. Later (I.7.46), Macbeth himself, in trying to deflect his wife's arguments, puts forward the view that in daring/doing

y

more than what is proper – or natural – for a man to do, one is no longer a man. Despite his argument, he, of course, goes on to do precisely that.

The letter to Lady Macbeth shows not only complete trust in his wife but also affection and love: 'my dearest partner of greatness' (lines 9–10) suggests a warm equality.

Scene 6

King Duncan arrives at Macbeth's castle with his two sons and attendant thanes. He admires the air. Lady Macbeth – without her husband – greets Duncan and they exchange pleasant courtesies. Duncan takes her hand and is led into the castle.

Comment

Once more the theme of reality versus appearances is lightly alluded to. The air and the castle appear delightful, but are in reality to be the site of foul murder.

Scene 7

Macbeth debates whether to murder King Duncan

As Macbeth's household prepares the feast for Duncan, Macbeth, alone, debates murdering him. The biggest problem as he sees it is that murdering his own liege, kinsman and guest would set a precedent that would return to plague him. Also, he cannot dismiss the fact that Duncan has been such a good king – heaven itself will expose the wickedness of Macbeth. The only justification for the murder is, finally, his own ambition. His wife enters and he tells her he intends to change his mind and not murder Duncan. She accuses him of cowardice. They argue but her violent resolution wins: she outlines the plan, and he agrees to it.

Comment

Macbeth reasons that if he could get away with the murder, then he wouldn't worry about damnation in the after-life. However, as he considers Duncan's virtuous qualities, pictures of angels and cherubim seeking revenge attack and frighten him. Again, **ironically** (see Literary Terms), the initial hope that one blow would end the matter (lines 4–5) turns out to be utterly false: the death of Duncan is swiftly followed by the 'execution' of the two innocent guards.

Lady Macbeth attacks her husband exactly where she knows it will hurt: his courage and manhood are at stake. And she does what she said she would do in Act I Scene 5, 'pour my spirits in thine ear' (lines 23–4). Her strength of purpose and her leadership offer a remarkable contrast to Macbeth's performance at this stage. Notice how his final words in this scene, 'False face must hide what the false heart doth know', echo Lady Macbeth's earlier advice (I.5.61–4).

Test (Act I)

a Fill in
the blanks

Three .... meet, and prepare to meet with .... Meanwhile a wounded captain tells King .... about the bravery of Macbeth and .... against the rebels led by the Thane of .... The King decides to reward Macbeth for his efforts, and orders .... to greet Macbeth with his new title, Thane of ....

The three .... surprise Macbeth and his friend as they return from the battlefield. They predict that Macbeth will be .... and that his friend's descendants will ascend the ....

On arriving at court, the King announces that his son, ... is heir apparent.

Lady Macbeth receives a .... from her husband. She calls on .... to give her strength to help persuade her husband to kill the King. Immediately the King has arrived at the castle .... succeeds in persuading Macbeth to murder him.

b Give modern words for these
words used by Shakespeare

1	kerns (I.2.13)	6	vantage (I.3.112)
2	chops (I.2.22)	7	fantastical (I.3.138)
3	memorize (I.2.41)	8	surmise (I.3.140)
4	Bellona (I.2.60)	9	metaphysical (I.5.27)
5	lapped (I.2.60)	10	sightless (I.7.23)

y   19

C Quiz

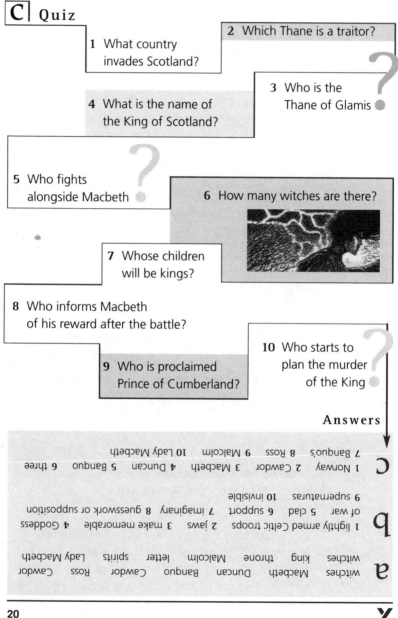

1 What country invades Scotland?

2 Which Thane is a traitor?

3 Who is the Thane of Glamis

4 What is the name of the King of Scotland?

5 Who fights alongside Macbeth

6 How many witches are there?

7 Whose children will be kings?

8 Who informs Macbeth of his reward after the battle?

9 Who is proclaimed Prince of Cumberland?

10 Who starts to plan the murder of the King

Answers

C 1 Norway   2 Cawdor   3 Macbeth   4 Duncan   5 Banquo   6 three
7 Banquo's   8 Ross   9 Malcolm   10 Lady Macbeth

b 1 lightly armed Celtic troops   2 jaws   3 make memorable   4 Goddess
of war   5 clad   6 support   7 imaginary   8 guesswork or supposition
9 supernaturas   10 invisible

a witches   Macbeth   Duncan   Banquo   Cawdor   Ross   Cawdor
witches   King   throne   Malcolm   letter   spirits   Lady Macbeth

Act II

Scene 1

Macbeth and Banquo meet briefly

Banquo is out walking late with his son, Fleance. He cannot sleep and feels something is wrong. He encounters Macbeth and presents him with a diamond for Macbeth's wife, a gift from the King. He tells Macbeth he dreamt of the witches. Macbeth dismisses thoughts of them, but suggests that he and Banquo speak about the matter another time. Banquo agrees. Macbeth is left alone and imagines he sees a dagger in front of him – a dagger which guides him towards killing Duncan. Initially he feels horror, but this gives way to resolution. As the bell rings, he determines to kill Duncan.

Comment

The introduction of Banquo at this point allows us another point of contrast with Macbeth. Banquo's dreams are invaded. Banquo senses something is wrong, but he does not know what. His openness in admitting his feelings is in stark contrast to Macbeth's flat lie that he doesn't think about the witches. The gift of the diamond, too, especially to Lady Macbeth, underlines the Macbeth's ingratitude, and highlights another **irony** (see Literary Terms): Duncan has again failed to read 'the mind's construction in the face' (I.4.12–14), for it is Lady Macbeth who has ensured he is to be killed.

Macbeth's request to talk of the witches later with its promise to 'make honour for you' (line 26) is an attempt to sound Banquo out. Banquo's answer, which insists on maintaining integrity, is unlikely to please Macbeth. Banquo cannot be bought. It is not surprising that later (III.1.55) Macbeth says he feels 'rebuked' by him.

Scene 2

Macbeth murders King Duncan

Nerves on edge, Lady Macbeth waits for Macbeth to return from having done the murder. Her mood is jubilant, and she boasts how she has drugged the guards. She would have murdered Duncan herself, but seeing him sleeping reminded her of her father.

Macbeth enters, shattered. He is carrying two bloodstained daggers. He is obsessed by the noises he has heard, and distressed by the fact that when passing Malcolm and Donalbain's chamber he was unable to say 'amen' in response to their request for blessing. The guilt of what he has done torments him, and Lady Macbeth attempts to allay his fears. She focuses on the need to keep to the plan of action – ordering him to go back and place the daggers beside the guards, so as to incriminate them. Macbeth, however, is too terrified to return. Lady Macbeth goes instead and leaves him there alone. A knocking at the castle gate further disturbs his state of mind. Lady Macbeth re-enters. As the knocking continues she advises that he pull himself together and that they retire to bed, so as not to be seen up and about when the murder is discovered.

Comment

We do not see the actual murder on stage. Instead, prior to the murder we are made aware of the vision of the dagger leading Macbeth on; and after the murder we are conscious of sounds which disturb the peace. We are meant to 'feel' the murder happening.

Lady Macbeth is clearly – despite some nervousness – entirely in control of herself and of her husband. She planned the execution, and now her readiness of mind and strength of purpose compensate for Macbeth's failure to act decisively once the murder is committed.

Irony (see Literary Terms) is ever present. Lady Macbeth imagines that washing one's hands will wash away guilt: it is she, finally (V.1.42), who is unable to wash her hands clean. And her comment to Macbeth, 'Infirm of purpose!' (line 52), comes back to haunt her, as he strengthens in evil resolve, whilst she becomes madly suicidal – anticipated in her dismissive comment 'so, it will make us mad' (line 34).

The fact that such a great warrior – and killer of men – is so lost in guilt indicates the extent of the evil Macbeth has committed. Earlier in the play, he wanted to 'jump the life to come' (I.7.7) – as if there were no divine retribution to worry about. Now, the need for 'amen', which he cannot speak and the fact that even the ocean cannot clean him, suggest a state of total damnation.

Scene 3

The knocking continues and a Porter, hungover from the night's feast, opens the gate. As he does so, he imagines he is the porter of Hell. He lets in Macduff and Lennox. Seemingly awoken by their knocking, Macbeth comes to greet them. Macduff asks to be led to the King. Lennox comments how stormy the night was. Macduff, discovering the murder, returns, loudly proclaiming

Scene 3

The murder of the King is discovered

treason. As Macduff wakes the castle, Macbeth and Lennox rush in to ascertain the facts for themselves. Lady Macbeth appears, then Banquo, and both are told of the reason for the commotion. Macbeth returns and bemoans the dreadful deed. At this point Malcolm and Donalbain arrive and are informed indirectly by Macbeth, then directly by Macduff, that their father has been murdered. Lennox suggests the guards may have been responsible, and it emerges that, on 'discovering' the murder, Macbeth had immediately killed them. Macduff questions this, and as Macbeth justifies his actions, his wife faints and attention is diverted to her. Banquo assumes command and directs them to meet in the hall. As they leave the stage, Malcolm and Donalbain remain: they decide to flee – suspecting treachery from someone closely related.

Comment

The grimness of the previous scene gives way to a brief comic interlude. Although the Porter is crude and rough, and his introduction is intended to make us laugh, he also performs other important functions. The knocking reminds us that we are still in the world where the Macbeths commit murder. Therefore, the Porter's self-appointed role as a Hell-porter is not so fanciful. Literally, it would seem, there is Hell where Macbeth is. And, more interestingly still, much of what the Porter says is connected to contemporary events: namely, the Gunpowder Plot and the scale of its treason. Thus, whilst including some jokes, the Porter's remarks widen the message of the play – Hell is not only on the stage in Macbeth's castle, but present in the society for which Shakespeare was writing. Furthermore, we should not forget that we know the murder has been committed – this delay in its discovery heightens the tension and our sense of anticipation.

Lennox's account of the storm receives an almost dismissive four-word reply (line 57) from Macbeth. Macbeth has no time for conversation – he is keyed up and waiting for the inevitable outburst from Macduff.

Typically, in a world of inverted values, Lady Macbeth's first concern on 'learning' that Duncan has been murdered is that it reflects badly on 'our house' (line 85). Equally typically, it is Banquo who provides a more sensitive perspective.

Macbeth's justification for killing the two guards becomes so colourful that he is in danger of being exposed through 'overacting' his part. Lady Macbeth's swoon, therefore, at this point conveniently distracts attention away from her husband.

Donalbain and Malcolm's decision to flee clearly plays into Macbeth's hands. However, that does not mean it was a bad decision. To have stayed may well have led to their own assassinations. As they observe, the 'nea'er in blood / The nearer bloody' (lines 137–8). This can only mean they suspect Macbeth.

Scene 4

Macbeth has been named King

Ross and an Old Man recall the dreadful night of the murder. The Old Man cannot remember a parallel to it. As they discuss the unnatural state of things, darkness seems to have taken the place of light. Macduff enters and brings them up to date with the news. Because they have fled, Duncan's sons are suspected of paying the guards to commit the murder. Macbeth has been named King and has gone to Scone to be crowned. Ross asks Macduff whether he will go to the ceremony. Macduff says he will not, but will return home to Fife. Ross intends to go. They part; the Old Man pronounces a blessing.

Test (Act II)

a | Fill in the blanks

Banquo is walking with his son, ... Macbeth meets them, and Banquo talks about his dream of the three Weird ....

Macbeth hesitates about killing ...., but as he moves towards ....'s chamber, he thinks he sees a .... leading him on.

He does not remove the murder .... from the scene and is too frightened to go back. .... mocks his cowardice. The sleeping .... are smeared with blood, so they appear to be guilty.

There is a knocking at the gate. .... and .... have arrived. .... and Lady Macbeth begin washing and changing their clothes.

Macbeth takes the visitors to the King's chamber, which .... enters alone. The murder is discovered and the alarm raised. During the commotion the guards are slain by .... and .... faints. .... and .... go to England and Ireland. .... will not attend Macbeth's coronation.

b | Give modern words for these words used by Shakespeare

1	largess (II.1.14)	6	incarnadine (II.2.62)
2	dudgeon (II.1.46)	7	Belzebub (II.3.4)
3	Hecate (II.1.52)	8	equivocate (II.3.10)
4	grooms (II.2.5)	9	auger-hole (II.3.119)
5	ravelled (II.2.37)	10	suborned (II.4.24)

C | Quiz

1 Who walks because he cannot sleep?

2 Where is Macbeth led by a dagger he sees?

3 What is it that summons Duncan to 'heaven or to hell'

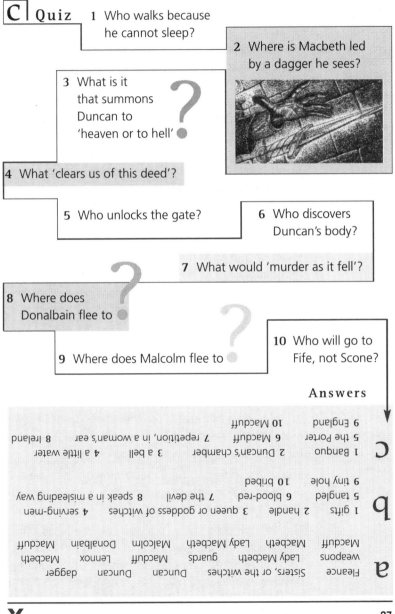

4 What 'clears us of this deed'?

5 Who unlocks the gate?

6 Who discovers Duncan's body?

7 What would 'murder as it fell'?

8 Where does Donalbain flee to

9 Where does Malcolm flee to

10 Who will go to Fife, not Scone?

Answers

C 1 Banquo 2 Duncan's chamber 3 a bell 4 a little water 5 the Porter 6 Macduff 7 repetition, in a woman's ear 8 Ireland 9 England 10 Macduff

b 1 gifts 2 handle 3 queen or goddess of witches 4 serving-men 5 tangled 6 blood-red 7 the devil 8 speak in a misleading way 9 tiny hole 10 bribed

a Fleance Sisters, or the witches Duncan Duncan dagger weapons Lady Macbeth Lennox Macduff guards Lady Macbeth Macbeth Malcolm Donalbain Macduff Macbeth Macduff

Act III

Scene 1

Banquo reflects on the witches' words

Banquo reflects on the witches' prophecies, and suspects that Macbeth did indeed obtain the crown through treachery. But the prophecies have all come true for Macbeth; he reasons there is hope for his family. Macbeth and Lady Macbeth and their entourage arrive. They remind Banquo he is the chief guest at their feast/banquet that evening. Macbeth pretends that he needs Banquo's advice on the following day on how to deal with Malcolm and Donalbain, who are abroad and spreading rumours. He discovers from Banquo details of his journey and that Fleance will be with him. Macbeth then dismisses everyone. Alone, he reveals that he fears Banquo, and that the thought of Banquo's offspring becoming kings is entirely unacceptable to him. Two murderers are brought in. He angrily explains to them why Banquo is their mutual enemy, and they agree to perform the murder.

Comment

The witches' prophecies have clearly disturbed Banquo's peace of mind, and although there is no suggestion that he will 'help' the prophecies come true (as Macbeth did), he nevertheless begins to believe they hold some 'truth'. This contrasts – in the same scene – with Macbeth's obsession that they will come true, and therefore that he (Macbeth) must stop them.

Macbeth's comments on Banquo later in this scene give us much information about the character of Banquo: what emerges is his courage, wisdom and integrity.

This is the first time we see Macbeth as King. Immediately we discover the kind of king he is going to be: entirely duplicitous – the appearance of an 'innocent flower', but really 'the serpent under't' (I.5.64–5).

Pretending to be friendly, Macbeth casually finds out Banquo's movements that night and confirms that Fleance will be with him. All this to entrap and murder him and his child.

The depths to which Macbeth has sunk are clear in his conversation with the murderers: here is a great warrior-hero – 'Bellona's bridegroom' (I.2.56) – who now has to meet the most vicious and corrupt kind of men in secret in order to both disguise and obtain his ends. The fact that he himself despises these men is shown in the way he addresses them – the interruption of the first murderer's solemn declaration of loyalty with the ironic 'Your spirits shine through you' (line 127) suggests contempt. Subsequently, the mission of the third murderer (III.3) shows how little Macbeth actually trusts the first two. But, then, trust is no longer something Macbeth believes in. Crucially, in the next scene (III.2), even Lady Macbeth is not told of his plans.

Scene 2

Macbeth will commit another crime

Lady Macbeth wants to speak to her husband before the feast. She is not happy – uncertainty and insecurity trouble them both. Macbeth appears and she upbraids him both for staying alone and for his continual dwelling on their actions. Macbeth envies the peaceful dead. Lady Macbeth attempts to cheer him up. They discuss the feast ahead, resolve to praise Banquo at it, and then Macbeth reveals his fear of Banquo and Fleance. He declares that he intends to commit another dreadful crime. He will not tell her what it is, but asks her to praise it when it has been achieved. Lady Macbeth is amazed but drawn along with him.

Comment

In the encounters so far, Lady Macbeth has been dominant. Now we see the situation changing. Macbeth is keeping himself to himself and brooding on the crimes committed, and on the crimes he intends to commit. Furthermore, he is not sharing his thoughts with his 'dearest partner of greatness' (I.5.9–10) and so she herself is feeling isolated. This despite the affectionate term – 'dearest chuck' (line 45) – Macbeth uses for her.

For Macbeth this proves a period in which he grows stronger – 'Things bad begun make strong themselves by ill' (line 55) – and becomes accustomed to doing evil; for Lady Macbeth it is the start of her disintegration – she will take control one more time, at the banquet (III.4), and then she will be overwhelmed by the tide of evil she has helped unleash, and go mad. Their roles are reversing.

Scene 3

The two murderers are joined by a third murderer. They await Banquo and Fleance's approach, spring out and manage to assassinate Banquo. In the confusion Fleance escapes. The murderers will inform Macbeth what has been done.

Scene 4

Banquo has been killed

Macbeth welcomes various guests to his banquet. The first murderer appears and Macbeth steps aside to speak with him. He learns that Banquo is dead, but that Fleance escaped – this disturbs him. He returns to the feast and is gently told off by his wife for his absence.

Banquo's ghost appears at the banquet

As he stands, making a speech praising Banquo, Banquo's ghost takes the only remaining chair. Only Macbeth can see the ghost and he is terrified. Lady Macbeth's quick thinking covers up the fact that Macbeth is beginning to reveal his guilt. The ghost disappears and Macbeth becomes calm again. Once more he attempts good cheer and invokes the name of

Banquo: the ghost reappears and Macbeth loses his nerve altogether. He recovers himself when the ghost disappears again, but too late for the banquet to continue. Lady Macbeth heads off a question from Ross and dismisses everyone. Alone with his wife, Macbeth confides that Macduff seems to be standing against him. He reveals, too, that he has spies everywhere, and that he intends to revisit the witches.

Comment   This scene raises the interesting question of witchcraft and psychology. Certainly, the supernatural is superbly developed: we have had the witches, their prophecies, the dagger that led Macbeth to Duncan, and now we have the ghost of Banquo. But whereas Banquo saw and heard the witches alongside Macbeth, here only Macbeth sees the vision. As Lady Macbeth says, 'When all's done / You look but on a stool' (line 66–7). This has practical implications for any production of the play – is the ghost in the mind of Macbeth solely (and so not shown on stage), or does a ghost really appear? Perhaps because of its sheer dramatic impact, most directors of the play tend to want to show the ghost!

The dramatic tension builds up in this scene. Firstly, the appearance of the murderer (albeit on the fringes) is itself shocking – perhaps one needs to consider this in modern terms: it would be like a street gangster appearing in the doorway of a State banquet. The risks to Macbeth in being seen with such a person are enormous – and this gives a clear indication of his state of mind. Macbeth *has* to know that Banquo and Fleance are dead, whatever the consequences. As he says later in the scene: 'For mine own good / All causes shall give way' (lines 134–5). Secondly, the tension is exploited by the way that Macbeth in fact reveals – almost plainly – his guilt, but on each occasion Lady Macbeth is able ingeniously to bale him out. We are kept on tenterhooks: will he be exposed?

The strain on Lady Macbeth is evident. Although he himself has been terrified, Macbeth, by the end of the scene, seems casual in his attitude to what has happened. His comment, 'We are yet but young in deed' (line 143) suggests that this mere blip will soon pass. She, however, has had to use all her resources and intelligence to contain the potential damage of exposure. Earlier she had said 'Naught's had, all's spent' (III.2.5) and we see this particularly in this scene: she wanted to be queen and the scene begins with her keeping 'her state' (line 5), in other words, remaining on her throne. If there was anywhere in the play where Lady Macbeth could enjoy being queen to the full, it is here: she is on her throne, surrounded by subjects. Yet, because of Macbeth's actions, this becomes a hollow and empty event, lacking any dignity or regal

Y

significance. Perhaps it is no surprise, then, that at this point she does begin to question the value of what has been accomplished. Macbeth, we notice, no longer talks of *we* – himself and his partner of greatness – but of himself alone: 'For mine own good / All causes shall give way' (lines 134–5).

Banquo's ghost, **ironically** (see Literary Terms), occupies Macbeth's seat – as his descendants will his throne – 'push us from our stools' (line 81).

The reference once more to sleep (line 140) reinforces our sense of the Macbeths' guilt, but also points to the **dramatic irony** (see Literary Terms) that Macbeth himself is a prophet: 'Macbeth shall sleep no more' (II.2.43).

Scene 5

The witches prepare to meet Macbeth again

The three witches enter and meet Hecate, the goddess of witchcraft, and their leader. She tells them off for not having included her in the dealings with Macbeth. She commands them to prepare a specially strong spell to delude Macbeth when he comes to meet them the following morning.

Scene 6

The political situation in Scotland

Lennox outlines to another lord in deeply **ironic** (see Literary Terms) terms his understanding of what has been happening in Scotland: i.e. that Macbeth is responsible for all the murders that have plagued the state. Malcolm is in the English court attempting to raise military support to reclaim his throne. Macduff is in disgrace for refusing to attend Macbeth's banquet and is trying to join Malcolm.

Test (Act III)

a Fill in the blanks

.... suspects that Macbeth has killed ....

.... However, Macbeth appears friendly towards him and invites him to be chief guest at his feast. At the same time he also sees two .... and persuades them that .... is their enemy. Macbeth does not involve .... in his plans.

Three murderers kill .... but his son ....
escapes.

Twice during the feast Macbeth sees ....
.... He is terrified. ....
prevents Macbeth blurting out the truth.

Later, Macbeth decides he will do two important things: he will visit .... and he will destroy
.... tells the .... to prepare for Macbeth's visit.Everyone is now beginning to suspect Macbeth. .... confides his suspicions to another lord. Meanwhile, ... has fled to England.

b Give modern words for these
words used by Shakespeare

1 all-thing (III.1.13)   6 shard-bone (III.2.42)
2 invention (III.1.32)   7 seeling (III.2.46)
3 genius (III.1.55)   8 ceremony (III.4.35)
4 unlineal (III.1.62)   9 flaws (III.4.62)
5 shoughs (III.1.93)   10 self-abuse (III.4.141)

C Quiz

1 Who is invited as chief guest to Macbeth's feast?

2 Which two people are blamed for the murder of Duncan?

3 How many murderers does Macbeth use to kill Banquo?

4 Who else does Macbeth instruct the murderers to kill?

5 Whose ghost haunts Macbeth?

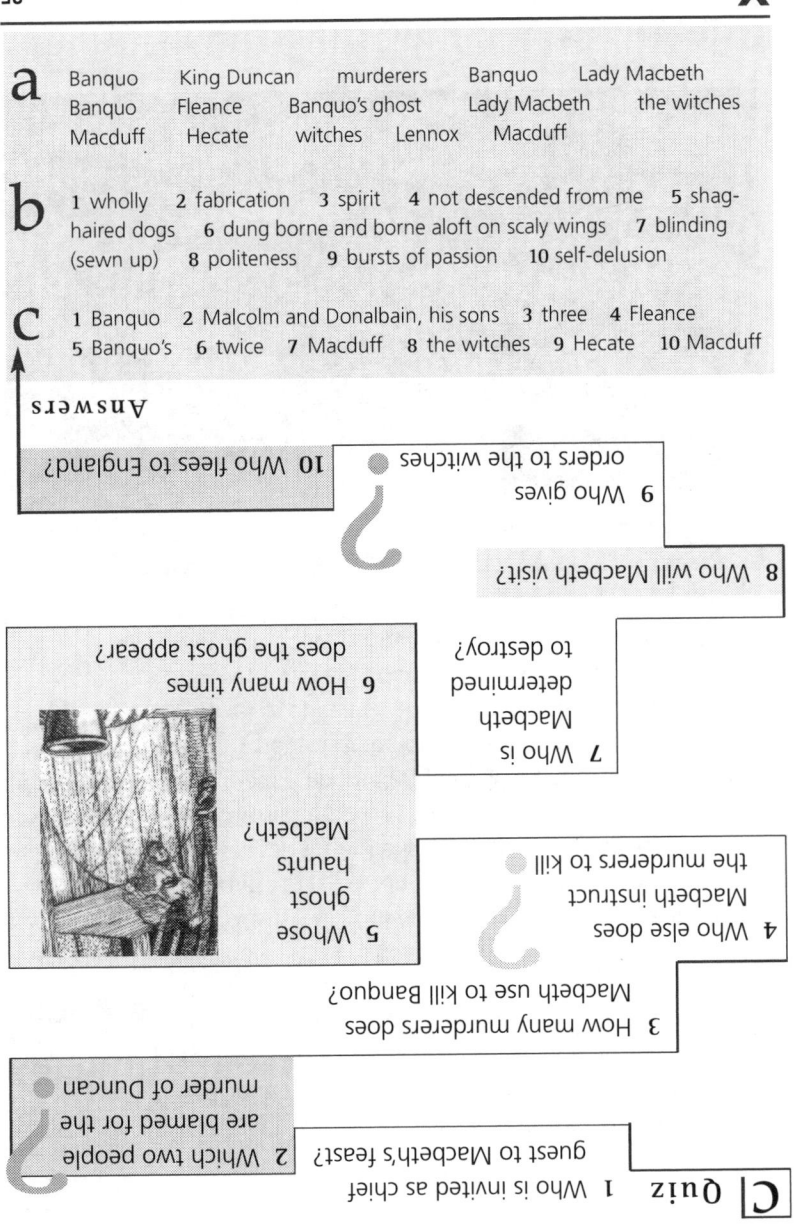

6 How many times does the ghost appear?

7 Who is Macbeth determined to destroy?

8 Who will Macbeth visit?

9 Who gives orders to the witches?

10 Who flees to England?

Answers

a   Banquo   King Duncan   murderers   Banquo   Lady Macbeth   Banquo   Fleance   Banquo's ghost   Lady Macbeth   the witches   Macduff   Hecate   witches   Lennox   Macduff

b   1 wholly   2 fabrication   3 spirit   4 not descended from me   5 shag-haired dogs   6 dung borne and borne aloft on scaly wings   7 blinding (sewn up)   8 politeness   9 bursts of passion   10 self-delusion

c   1 Banquo   2 Malcolm and Donalbain, his sons   3 three   4 Fleance   5 Banquo's   6 twice   7 Macduff   8 the witches   9 Hecate   10 Macduff

Act IV

Scene 1

Macbeth meets the witches again; they prophesy three things

Three witches cast a spell and prepare to meet Macbeth. Hecate and three other witches appear and Hecate approves the work of the first three witches, and then disappears with the three she has brought with her. Macbeth enters and commands them to answer his questions. They call up powerful spirits to respond to him. He is told three prophecies: that he should fear Macduff, that he cannot be harmed by one born of a woman, and that he is secure until Birnan Wood comes to Dunsinane. He then presses them for more information about Banquo's offspring and is shocked to see a vision of eight kings all descended from Banquo, who also appears. The witches suddenly vanish and Macbeth curses them. Lennox arrives and informs Macbeth that Macduff has fled to England. Macbeth decides to kill Macduff's wife and children.

Comment	The supernatural atmosphere is charged with evil. The witches' spells are particularly nauseating in their graphic detail – here is evidence of precisely how unnatural these hags are.

Before his arrival, Macbeth is described as 'Something wicked' (line 45) – not even someone. Macbeth is one of their kind now.

Earlier uncertainties have been stripped away. At their first meeting (I.3) the witches informed him of the prophecies; now he demands of them what he wants to know. He even threatens the powerful master spirits with a curse if they do not answer him (line 104). And when he leaves, there is no more agonising about what he needs to do – or discussing the situation with his wife – Macduff's castle is to be attacked. Macbeth has fallen to extraordinary depths – he will murder women and children without a second thought.

One reason why Macbeth trusts the prophecies is that they come true so quickly: now, having been told to watch out for Macduff, Lennox appears with the same warning. The **irony** (see Literary Terms) is that all the prophecies are double-edged and turn against him. Banquo's comment accurately reflects the truth: 'The instruments of darkness tell us truths; / Win us with honest trifles, to betray's / In deepest consequence' (I.3.123–5). These words are prophetic and condemn all that Macbeth comes to believe.

Two or three horsemen bring Macbeth word that Macduff has fled – the spies he has 'fee'd' (III.4.131).

Scene 2	Lady Macduff is with her son and Ross. Ross informs her that her husband has fled to England. Lady Macduff accuses her husband of cowardice. Ross makes his

Lady Macduff and her son are attacked

excuses and leaves. The son interrogates his mother about the meaning of the word traitor. A messenger abruptly arrives, warns of danger, and leaves. Murderers enter, kill her son, and pursue her to kill her too.

Scene 3

Malcolm and Macduff discuss kingship

In England Malcolm entertains Macduff: he is testing his integrity because, with all the spies and traitors that Macbeth has created, he is afraid he might be on Macbeth's side. Malcolm pretends that he is even more depraved than Macbeth, and so should not ascend the throne. Macduff's lament for Scotland, however, convinces Malcolm – who then retracts his confessions of evil – that Macduff is sincere and opposed to Macbeth. He reveals to Macduff that he has English support for an invasion of Scotland. Macduff is confused but pleased by this turn of events. A doctor appears and mentions the saintly work of King Edward the Confessor. After he leaves, Malcolm and Macduff discuss the true virtues of kingship, and how this is passed on to succeeding monarchs. Ross arrives with news and eventually, reluctantly, informs Macduff that his family has been murdered. Macduff is temporarily overwhelmed by the news, but pulls himself together. He will support Malcolm and vows that he will kill Macbeth himself.

Comment

This scene provides a balance to the others in Act IV. The evil of Macbeth's visit to the witches and the dreadful murder of the Macduffs now give way to more 'normal' emotions and reactions. Malcolm is suspicious of Macduff – neither of them at the beginning of the scene know what Macbeth has done to Macduff's family. One cause of Malcolm's suspicion is, as he says, 'He hath not touched you yet' (line 14), meaning that Macbeth has not injured Macduff's family (a **dramatic irony** – see Literary Terms – as the audience has seen the preceding scene), and so why should Macduff quarrel with Macbeth? Malcolm has already experienced traitors who have tried to entrap him (lines 117–20), and so is wary of committing himself.

This scene is full of dramatic tension – Malcolm plays his game with Macduff, Ross is reluctant to reveal the truth – but is a scene of words, not actions. So it is a springboard into Act V. Equally, it is important in the number of dramatic contrasts it provides. The contrast between King Macbeth and King Edward is key. Also, we should bear in mind here that Malcolm will be king – and we see the kind of man he is, the values he possesses, and we are reminded how good Duncan was. This scene, therefore, does explore the issues of kingship. Another personal contrast should be noted: Macduff's reaction to the death of his wife can be compared with Macbeth's reaction (V.5.17–27). Such a contrast will show how desensitised Macbeth has become to all normal human feeling.

The reference to the way a monarch might cure the King's Evil (Scrofula) with a touch and how this gift is passed on was surely present not only to contrast with Macbeth's cursed reign, but also to please King James, who saw himself as having this gift.

Test (Act IV)

a Fill in the blanks

Macbeth visits the ..witches.. and also meets their
..masters.. . He learns that the one man he should fear
is called Macduff. but that nothing can harm
Macbeth until .Birnan. .Wood.. comes to
Dunsinane. . He is pleased with this. He is not so
pleased to learn that Banquo's descendants will
be kings.

On leaving, Macbeth discovers that Macduff.. has fled
to England. He orders his enemy's family to be destroyed.
..Ross.. warns Lady Macduff... but she and
her ....Son... are both murdered.

In England, ..Macduff. visits Malcom at the court of
the English king. ..Ross.. also arrives to tell
Macduff that his family has been slaughtered.
Malcom.. informs them that England will provide
an army, led by ..Syward., to defeat Macbeth. .
..Macduff vows to kill Macbeth.

b Give modern words for these words used by Shakespeare

1 brinded (IV.1.1)
2 drab (IV.1.31)
3 chaudron (IV.1.33)
4 bodements (IV.1.95)
5 enow (IV.2.57)

6 shag-haired (IV.2.84)
7 rawness (IV.3.26)
8 affeered (IV.3.34)
9 confineless (IV.3.55)
10 fee-grief (IV.3.196)

C | Quiz

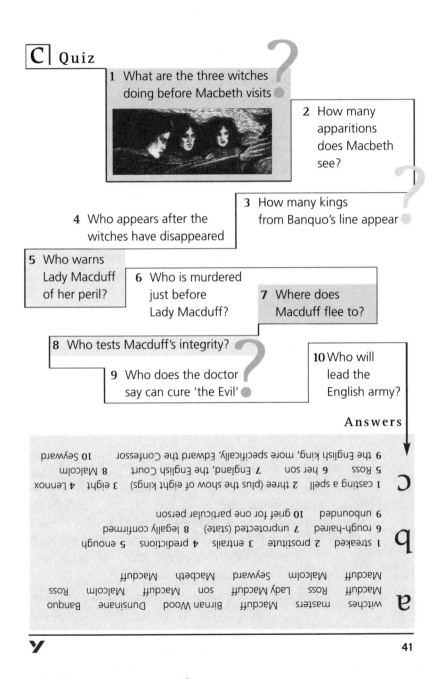

1 What are the three witches doing before Macbeth visits

2 How many apparitions does Macbeth see?

3 How many kings from Banquo's line appear

4 Who appears after the witches have disappeared

5 Who warns Lady Macduff of her peril?

6 Who is murdered just before Lady Macduff?

7 Where does Macduff flee to?

8 Who tests Macduff's integrity?

9 Who does the doctor say can cure 'the Evil'

10 Who will lead the English army?

Answers

C 1 casting a spell 2 three (plus the show of eight kings) 3 eight 4 Lennox 5 Ross 6 her son 7 England, the English Court 8 Malcolm 9 the English king, more specifically, Edward the Confessor 10 Seyward

b 1 streaked 2 prostitute 3 entrails 4 predictions 5 enough 6 rough-haired 7 unprotected (state) 8 legally confirmed 9 unbounded 10 grief for one particular person

a witches   masters   Macduff   Birnan Wood   Dunsinane   Banquo
Macduff   Ross   Lady Macduff   son   Macduff   Malcolm   Ross
Macduff   Malcolm   Seyward   Macbeth   Macduff

Act V

Scene 1

Lady
Macbeth
reveals her
guilt while
asleep

In Macbeth's castle at Dunsinane a doctor and a waiting-gentlewoman discuss their patient, Lady Macbeth. The woman refuses to repeat what she has heard Lady Macbeth say in her sleep, since she has no witness to corroborate her statements. As the doctor tries to persuade her, Lady Macbeth appears, sleepwalking. They hear her reveal her guilt and watch her try to remove blood from her hands. The doctor concludes that she is in need of spiritual rather than medical attention.

Comment

The clear mental breakdown of Lady Macbeth is both deeply upsetting and, in psychological terms, profoundly true. As with all guilt, there is an obsession with the past. Remember, it was Lady Macbeth who said, 'what's done is done' (III.2.12), suggesting that it would no longer be of concern. Here, despite her courage, ambition and strength of purpose, all that has been 'done' is not past, but present – and ever-present – in her mind. She refers to her earlier declaration when she says, 'What's done cannot be undone' (lines 63–4). The contrast with Macbeth himself is clear – 'I cannot taint with fear' (V.3.3). Until the prophecies start unravelling, Macbeth seems not to worry.

There is **dramatic irony** (see Literary Terms) in the fact that physical symptoms of her guilt include the attempt to wash clean her hands. We link this to both her statement that 'a little water clears us of this deed' (II.2.67) and Macbeth's insight upon actually committing the murder that 'Will all great Neptune's ocean wash this blood / Clean from my hand? No' (II.2.60–1).

Most of the play is written in **blank verse** (see Literary Terms). Notable exceptions are the Porter's scene (II.3)

y

and this appearance of Lady Macbeth. Before, particularly in the first two Acts, Lady Macbeth's speech had been blazing, fiery blank verse – the strong rhythms reflecting her strong grasp on reality, and her determination. Now, she speaks in **prose** (see Literary Terms) – choppy, abrupt, lurching from one incident to another, and even descending to **doggerel** (see Literary Terms) with the rhyme of Fife and wife (line 41). Shakespeare's writing brilliantly recreates what it means to 'break down' – the language is 'breaking down' as a result of the strain she is under. It is therefore not surprising that she commits suicide – she can no longer hold 'it' together, and on death, language disappears altogether. Note the contrast between the English court where the King heals 'Evil', and here where the disease is beyond any doctor's abilities.

Scene 2

Macbeth's enemies prepare to fight

Malcolm is marching north with a troop of English soldiers. We see the rebel Scottish powers who are determined to overthrow Macbeth. They plan to meet up with the English at Birnan Wood. The thanes comment on how uneasy Macbeth must feel, as his inadequacies and guilt must face the test; they are confident of victory.

Scene 3

Macbeth is not afraid

Macbeth enters with the doctor and attendants. He is in a fearless mood: the prophecies give him complete confidence that he is unassailable. He abuses a servant who reports that the English troops are arriving. Macbeth orders his armour and asks the doctor to cure his wife. He curtly dismisses the doctor's medical advice and asks him what would cure his country. But he scarcely listens to the reply – his mind is full of the prophecies, which alone guarantee his security.

Scene 4

Birnan Wood moves ...

Malcolm orders each of his men to cut down a branch from Birnan Wood and carry it in front of them so Macbeth will not know how many men are approaching. They learn that Macbeth intends to remain in Dunsinane – his strategy is to endure a siege. This is his only hope, as his troops are demoralised and fight because they are forced to, not because they are committed to him.

Scene 5

Lady Macbeth dies

Macbeth enters boasting that his castle can easily endure a siege: he is confident of victory. He is sorry he cannot go out to face the traitors – too many have deserted his army. A woman's scream is heard and Seyton goes to investigate. Macbeth reflects that nothing terrifies him now. Seyton returns and tells Macbeth his wife has died. For him this is a confirmation that life is meaningless. A messenger arrives and informs him that Birnan Wood is moving towards Dunsinane Castle. Outraged, and in some doubt about his destiny and the meaning of the prophecies, Macbeth immediately changes his strategy and orders an attack.

Scene 6

Macbeth kills Young Seyward

Malcolm, Macduff and Seyward with their army under camouflage approach Macbeth's castle. Battle commences. Macbeth is trapped but unbeaten. He encounters Young Seyward and kills him in combat. Meanwhile, Macduff seeks out Macbeth alone. Seyward invites Malcolm to take the castle.

Macbeth sees he has lost but will not contemplate suicide. At this point he encounters Macduff. Initially, he refuses to fight Macduff, but Macduff insists. As they fight, Macbeth mocks Macduff – no man born of a woman can defeat him. However, his confidence evaporates when Macduff informs him he was not 'born', but delivered by a Caesarean operation. Macbeth is suddenly afraid and refuses to fight. He realises the prophecies have betrayed him. Macduff now baits Macbeth. In a final act of courage Macbeth fights acduff and is killed. The battle has been won by Malcolm. Seyward – through Ross – discovers his son is dead. Macduff arrives with Macbeth's head, and hails Malcolm King of Scotland. Malcolm gives thanks by promoting the thanes to earls. He intends to put right the evil caused by Macbeth and invites everyone to his coronation at Scone.

Macduff kills Macbeth

Malcolm is King of Scotland

Comment Young Seyward is not a significant character, but his killing by Macbeth reminds us that Macbeth is, perhaps first and foremost, a warrior. Early in the play we hear of his ferocious credentials as a fighter – if we have forgotten about this, because subsequently Macbeth operates through murderers, then in this final scene we recall where his true strength is. This is important – otherwise Macduff's achievement in killing him in one-to-one combat is diminished.

The fact that Macbeth is primarily a warrior is also important in our final evaluation of him: because he succumbs to the temptation offered by the witches' words, the witches succeed in destroying almost every aspect of his true humanity. Even his courage temporarily deserts him (line 61) when he learns from Macduff how misleading the prophecies are – yet his courage returns: he will not yield. He will, as it were, take on Fate as well as Macduff – 'Yet I will try the last' (line 71) – and this, while it does not excuse his crimes, does enable us to see some remnant of his great bravery.

Macbeth's analysis of the witches' prophecies comes full circle: he was warned by Banquo (I.3.121–5) and now he has experienced and knows exactly what Banquo predicted. **Ironically** (see Literary Terms), just as Macbeth betrayed Duncan, so the witches have betrayed Macbeth. Considering the pros and cons of treason and murder, Macbeth commented 'we but teach / Bloody instructions, which, being taught, return / To plague the inventor' (I.7.8–10). This, too, has come true – he has had no rest as his own men and thanes have constantly deserted his cause, and his ultimate trust in the witches also turns out to be misplaced.

Malcolm's crowning concludes the play, but one important prophecy is still unfulfilled: that Banquo's children will attain the throne. The ending of the play can be interpreted in two different ways. First, a joyous occasion on which innocent, honest Malcolm will make good the wrongs during his reign. Second, some productions that see the evil commenced by the witches as so far-reaching that another alternative is possible: a cold, calculating King Malcolm surveys his victory – seeing Fleance in his army – and realises he must assassinate Fleance if he is to remain King.

Test (Act V)

a Fill in the blanks

.... is attended by a gentlewoman and doctor. Meanwhile, the .... army marches on Macbeth, who prepares for a siege. .... orders the boughs of trees to be cut down and used as camouflage.

.... hears a scream and learns that his wife has died. Macbeth continues with his preparations until he learns that .... is coming to ....

His army is losing, but Macbeth himself seems invulnerable. He kills .... in combat and then .... enters.

Macbeth initially doesn't want to fight him, but soon becomes confident. This lasts until he discovers that .... is not .... of .... At this point he realises that the prophecies have misled him, and he refuses to fight. .... accuses him of cowardice.

Macbeth's head is presented to .... who is acclaimed King of Scotland.

b Give modern words for these words used by Shakespeare

1 perturbation (V.1.9)
2 mated (V.1.74)
3 mortified (V.2.5)
4 pestered (V.2.23)
5 sway (V.3.9)

6 dis-seat (V.3.21)
7 dareful (V.5.6)
8 pull (V.5.42)
9 avouches (V.5.47)
10 undeeded (V.6.30)

C Quiz

1 Who will not speak 'having no witnesses to confirm' what she says?

2 Who constantly washes her hands

3 Where is Macbeth preparing for a siege?

4 What must every English soldier cut down and carry before him

5 Who informs Macbeth his queen is dead?

6 Whom must Macbeth fear?

7 Who does Macbeth first kill in combat?

9 Where are young Seyward's 'hurts'

8 Who kills Macbeth?

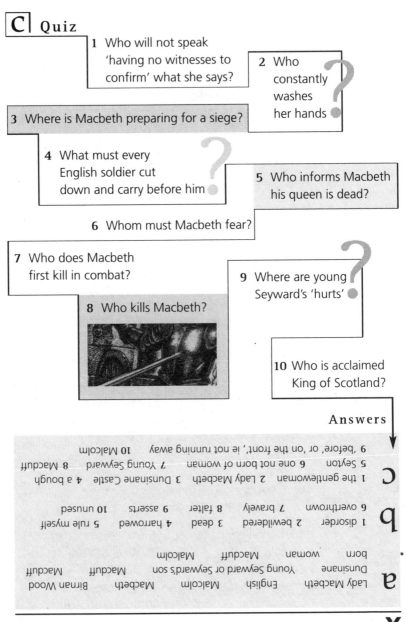

10 Who is acclaimed King of Scotland?

Answers

C
1 the gentlewoman   2 Lady Macbeth   3 Dunsinane Castle   4 a bough
5 Seyton   6 one not born of woman   7 Young Seyward   8 Macduff
9 'before' or 'on the front', ie not running away   10 Malcolm

b
1 disorder   2 bewildered   3 dead   4 harrowed   5 rule myself
6 overthrown   7 bravely   8 falter   9 asserts   10 unused

a
Lady Macbeth   English   Malcolm   Macbeth   Birnan Wood
Dunsinane   Young Seyward or Seyward's son   Macduff   Macduff   Macbeth
born woman   Macduff   Malcolm

48

Commentary

Themes

There are many themes in *Macbeth*. These include: good and evil, loyalty and love, hypocrisy and deception, justice and revenge, relationships, kingship, corruption, the supernatural. Central to the play is the theme of ambition.

Ambition

Ambition is the driving force of Macbeth's life. It is the theme (in this play) that sums up the Shakespearean idea of tragedy. 'Tragedy' usually concerns a great person – the hero – who through some weakness of character falls from grace, endures intense sufferings, and inevitably dies. If we consider what Macbeth's weakness is, we realise it is ambition.

Macbeth says: 'I have no spur ... but only / Vaulting ambition' (I.7.25–7). This comes after he has considered all the good reasons for not murdering Duncan – only ambition is left. Whilst the influence of both Lady Macbeth and the witches is strong, their power over Macbeth is only possible because the ambition is already there. Macbeth is a hero but one who is fatally undermined by his ambition: it is his ambition that leads the witches to Macbeth, and it is ambition that leads Macbeth to the deepest evil.

The supernatural

The supernatural, and witchcraft in particular, are also important. The presence of the supernatural in the play raises all sorts of questions concerning reality and appearances. Do witches really exist and have such powers? Did Shakespeare believe in them?

In Shakespeare's time witchcraft was a substantial issue: most people, including James I himself believed in witchcraft. The witches, then, are a real presence in the play, but we must remember that Macbeth is a free agent and has free will. He has chosen his course of action, and each subsequent action reinforces that original, and bad, choice. Macbeth is not forced to commit evil acts – he chooses his own damnation.

Characters

Macbeth

Ambitious

Brave

Treacherous

Murderous

Imaginative

Macbeth is a man of action: the play concerns the things he does. He is a fearless warrior – and an important lord – who defends his king against treachery. However, ambition is his fatal weakness. He is too easily influenced in the direction that he secretly desires to go.

Initially he has a conscience and a highly developed imagination – he sees all too well in his mind the horrors of what he is proposing to do – but he shuts out the implications of what this is telling him. His conscience leads to his moments of weakness – before and after murdering Duncan, and in seeing Banquo's ghost. Manhood is important to Macbeth. Lady Macbeth appeals to his manhood when persuading him to murder Duncan in the first place; she also makes a similar appeal during the banquet scene. Macbeth has a profound need to prove himself, which he identifies with being 'manly'. Physically, Macbeth is strong; emotionally and spiritually he proves weak and corruptible.

Lady Macbeth thinks him 'too full o'the milk of human-kindness' (I.5.15) – an extraordinary statement in the light of the murders Macbeth commits. But Macbeth

y

develops and changes. When the play starts he is a god-like hero – a firm, strong, loyal character. But he becomes 'this tyrant' (IV.3.12 – Malcolm), this 'dwarfish thief' (V.2.22 – Angus), this 'hellhound' (V.6.42 – Macduff), and finally 'this dead butcher' (V.6.108).

Lady Macbeth

Dominant
Practical
Cunning
Determined
Dependent
Haunted

Lady Macbeth's role is vital. Macbeth is tempted to do evil and Lady Macbeth is the key human agent – the one Macbeth trusts and loves – who ensures his temptation is complete. She is not, of course, a hero herself. She collapses once Macbeth withdraws his confidence from her: she wants to support her husband, but she has no further role to play in his life. Thus, she breaks down.

Lady Macbeth is determined that her husband should ascend the throne. We understand that Macbeth has 'deep desires', but these seem tame compared with Lady Macbeth's unquenchable aspirations: within 40 lines of appearing, she is summoning spirits into her body and soul! When Macbeth falters, she is there – and has the courage – to return the daggers, to faint at the news (and so divert attention from her husband), and to dismiss the guests from the banquet.

She is practical – she plans the details of the murder – and she has the future worked out. She is pre-eminently cunning.

However, like Macbeth, Lady Macbeth shows moments of humanity – she would have killed Duncan herself only he reminded her of her own father. She is not as cold and inhuman as she pretends to be. And this of course makes her breakdown seem inevitable. Ultimately, water will not wash away the stain of blood. By the end of the play she is recognised for what she is, a 'fiend-like queen' (V.6.108).

Finally, it is important to note that Shakespeare seems to draw the characters of Macbeth and Lady Macbeth very much as a linked pair: when Macbeth is weak, Lady Macbeth is strong; when Macbeth is callous and determined, she is tormented and disintegrating.

Duncan

Kind
Generous
Statesmanlike
Regal
Honest
Trusting

Duncan sets the standard for what a king should be. Macbeth in comparison is a very bad king, although ironically Macbeth aspires to be a king like Duncan, for he admires him.

Duncan is open, honest and honourable. He seems to enjoy the achievements of others and he generously offers them gifts. It is awful to reflect that our final view of Duncan is of him kissing (I.6) his hostess, Lady Macbeth, to whom he later sends a diamond as a present (II.1).

He seems decisive, and clearly inspires loyalty in his thanes. If he has a weakness it is a consequence of his goodness – his trust. Trusting Macbeth, he too readily steps into his castle without appropriate protection.

Banquo

Banquo begins his place in the story running parallel with Macbeth: they are both worthy thanes, both great warriors, both loyal to the King. Most importantly, they both meet the witches and hear their prophecies. Their reaction to these prophecies provides the starkest contrasts between Macbeth and Banquo.

Banquo is courageous and loyal. He possesses a wisdom and judgement borne out by events and acknowledged even by Macbeth. Banquo notes Macbeth's reaction to the prophecies, spotting the 'fear'. He commands the

Brave
Loyal
Honourable
Wise
Perceptive
Sensitive

witches to address him. Importantly, he sees precisely how dangerous such prophecies might be. Whereas Macbeth is immediately tempted by the witches' words, Banquo resists them. Banquo is man of integrity – a man who has chosen to do good, whatever the cost.

If there is a weakness in Banquo's character it might be his failure to act. Why does he not reveal what he knows about the prophecies immediately following the murder of Duncan? He suspects Macbeth, and failure to act on his suspicions costs him his life. Like Duncan, Banquo appears too trusting.

Macduff

Strong
Suspicious
Brave
Open
Loyal
Forthright

Fittingly, it is Macduff who discovers Duncan's murdered body, and becomes his avenger. He is a man of strong and emotional convictions. From the start he is suspicious of Macbeth. Later he refuses to attend the banquet, and this leads to the murder of his family. In this and in his flight to England we see what Malcolm calls 'this noble passion / Child of integrity' (IV.3.114–15). However, these acts also lead us to question his judgement. Was he right to flee to England? In his passion for justice, he is swept along in the train of events and fails to foresee the extent of savagery that Macbeth will exercise on his family.

One thing is clear – his deep and passionate attachment to and love for his family. His reaction to their deaths is one of the most moving scenes in the play. Haunted by their ghosts, he is determined to kill Macbeth. Macduff confronts his enemy and proves his courage and his strength.

Malcolm and Donalbain

King Duncan's sons flee after their father's death, and we meet only Malcolm again. Their presence together, though, particularly praying as Macbeth is committing the murder, reinforces our sense of brotherly love and of a close-knit family unit. Duncan isn't only a good king, but also a good family man. Malcolm seems similar to his father. The testing of Macduff shows a desire to want to penetrate beyond appearances to what someone really believes. He is dignified, determined, brave, recognises the worth of others, and can take advice. These qualities bode well for his future reign.

Lady Macduff

She appears in only one scene. But we notice her anger, her intelligence and her courage. There is a sharp contrast between the Lady Macduff scene and Macbeth's 'family' scenes with his wife.

Ross

Ross is mostly a messenger, albeit a highly ranked one.

Lennox

Lennox is a courtier who suspects Macbeth early on, and when he can, he switches sides to fight against Macbeth.

Seyward

Seyward is a fine soldier, who leads the English army. In a moving scene, he learns of the death of his son.

The Old Man

The Old Man is a typical Shakespearean creation. He acts as a chorus or commentary on the action: his age gives him the right to comment on exactly how unnatural the proceedings have been.

The Porter

The Porter is a marvellous lowlife type of character – drunk, obscene, talkative. Cleverly, Shakespeare bends even the Porter's language to reflect the themes of the play – whilst at the same time giving Macbeth an opportunity to wash and change clothing before reappearing on stage.

The witches

It can be argued that the witches are not human at all, and therefore cannot be considered to have characters. They are certainly a malign force in the play. They do not invite Macbeth to murder Duncan or even suggest such a thing. They symbolise evil, but man is free to resist them. Macbeth's downfall occurs partly because he comes to depend upon their information.

Shakespeare's Language

Shakespeare basically uses three styles of writing in his dialogue: poetic verse, **blank verse** and **prose** (see Literary Terms).

Poetic verse

Your face, my thane, is as a book where men
May read strange matters. To beguile the time,
Look like the time, bear welcome in your eye,
Your hand, your tongue; look like the innocent flower,
But be the serpent under't. He that's coming
Must be provided for; and you shall put
This night's great business into my dispatch,
Which shall to all our days and nights to come
Give solely sovereign sway and masterdom.

Here Lady Macbeth is taking charge of the situation in powerful poetic language. Though it is laid out as poetry it is phrased as though it is spoken with urgency – notice the short clear instructions. The use of poetry to convey her ideas is particularly sinister since the words she uses are as two-faced as she wants her husband to be. Duncan must be 'provided for' – not with good food and comfortable accommodation, but with a dagger!

Blank verse

Blank verse does not rhyme, except in the last two lines of a speech where an emphasis may be required or to round off a scene. It has the same rhythm or metre of five **iambs** (see Literary Terms) and is close to the stresses of spoken English.

Prose

Prose is most often given to minor or comic characters. Sometimes it is used to develop the plot or to give important information. The Porter's speech (III.1) introduces a grim humour since the drunken Porter pretends to be working at the gate of Hell admitting newcomers. Coming as it does immediately after the murder of Duncan, Macbeth's castle has truly become a Hell.

Key stage 3 & Shakespeare

Examinations

Every Year 9 pupil in Britain has to sit Key Stage 3 examinations in English, Mathematics and Science.

There are two English papers:

Paper I Reading and Writing Test (1 hour 30 minutes plus 15 minutes' reading time)

Paper II Shakespeare Test (1 hour 15 minutes)

We are not concerned here with Paper I so we shall concentrate upon the Shakespeare requirements.

Three plays are offered each year for study. Each play has two Key Scenes which are the subject of the examination paper. Your teacher will choose which play to study and more than likely the one Key Scene you will have to answer a question on. For the purposes of the examination you will be issued with a booklet containing all six scenes (two from each play), which you can take with you into the examination. There will be a task on each of the scenes and you will have to complete one of these tasks in the time available.

Read the tasks carefully: they give you a clear structure to use in your written response.

A typical question has three parts:

✴ A brief description of the scene you have studied
✴ Details of the task you have to complete
✴ Some prompts to help you arrange your thoughts

Act I.6–7: Macbeth is deciding whether to murder Duncan. Write the arguments for and against the murder. Think about:

• Duncan's attitude to Macbeth and to his wife

• Macbeth's relationship to Duncan

• Lady Macbeth's understanding of Macbeth's nature

Careful reading

First read the paper calmly and carefully. Take your time over this otherwise you may miss something very obvious – and discover too late that you have been answering the wrong question. It is a good idea to write the task down as the title of your essay on the top of your answer paper, so that it is always there as you are writing and reminds you to keep on the subject.

Using the prompts

Next write notes beside each of the prompts you have been given to help in your response. You could answer the task without bothering about the prompts – but the mark scheme below will make quite plain how important they really are! The prompts are there to help.

In Key Stage 3, the examiners really are your friends! They know this is the first time you will have sat a public examination on Shakespeare and that you will be nervous, so they are not trying to catch you out!

The mark scheme

You may be surprised to learn that the mark scheme for each question is identical. No matter which play you write about, your performance has to be measured against everyone else's and this would be impossible if there were six different mark schemes. What the examiner is looking for is the way you have answered the question you attempted.

A typical mark scheme

Achievement in Key Stage 3 is measured in terms of Levels, ranging from 1 up to 7, with 5 considered as the national average.

It is worth looking at the five statements that a mark scheme uses to describe Level 5 achievement:

✳ Answer selects *some appropriate moments* from the extract, and the significance of *some of these* is clearly explained

✳ *Some use of quotation*, though the answer may tend to present a general argument rather than a detailed account

✳ Points made will *generally be quite straightforward* ones

✳ *Some attempt* to link together points to form a coherent argument

✳ All of the prompts are referred to, but *one or more may not be covered in sufficient depth*

The italicised portions of the mark schemes are the important parts which the examiner will apply to your answer. If you put all these together, you might end up with this description of your essay:

The candidate knows the scene quite well and has used a few quotations which provide a general answer to the task though some parts are not covered very carefully.

The object of this Note on *Macbeth* is:

✳ To help you understand the play

✳ To enable you to answer the questions successfully

Success at Key Stage 3

The key to success is to enjoy the play. This enjoyment comes from hard work. You must first understand precisely what happens in the scene you are studying. Shakespeare's language can be a little complicated but it is English and it all makes sense.

The first step is to read the scene quite quickly and get

a rough idea of what happens. Then go through it more slowly getting a general idea of what each speech is about. If you have difficulties with phrases here and there, don't worry, the important thing is to get the gist of what each speech is about.

A good idea as you are studying is to listen to the words being spoken by a professional actor. Follow the scene in your book as the video or audiotape is being played. Or ask your teacher to read the speech out loud for you. When you hear Shakespeare read aloud by someone who understands it, you will discover that your only problems are individual and unfamiliar words.

Now that you have read and understood what is happening in the chosen scene, you must consider what important aspects of the play are revealed in it.

Examiners do not randomly select scenes for special study: they look for those which are important in particular ways. For Key Stage 3, there are four important aspects which apply to a Shakespearean play:

* The way ideas are presented
* The motivation and behaviour of characters
* The way the plot is developed
* The impact the lines make on the audience

The way ideas are presented

There are many different ways of presenting ideas. Among other topics, the play *Macbeth* explores the notion of kingship. We may be invited to consider this when characters discuss the qualities needed in a king (IV.3). At other times the contrast between a good king (Duncan) and a bad king (Macbeth) tells us about kingship without the idea being explicitly talked about by the characters in the play.

The motivation and behaviour of characters

It is often said that we are very good at understanding what makes other people tick, but find it harder to understand what motivates us. But the business of what makes people tick is what we are concerned with in understanding characters' motivation and behaviour.

For instance, Macbeth's desire to be king, and later to retain power, is what leads him to commit evil acts. How does Shakespeare show Macbeth's motivation and how it affects his behaviour and even his character?

The way the plot is developed

Shakespeare is a very accomplished storyteller. We take that for granted. But think for a moment about the art of telling a story. If it was entirely predictable, a story would surely be quite boring. After all, part of the interest of a story is not quite knowing where it is going next or how things will finally turn out.

Consider the prophecies made by the witches. How do events prove these to be correct? By doing this, you are seeing the way the plot develops.

The impact the lines make on the audience

Here you are asked to consider your reaction to what is said on stage. Shakespeare was a great writer: nothing is done accidentally. He uses language in two ways: to reflect the speaker's personality, and to create an impression in the audience's mind.

Talking of her own baby, Lady Macbeth says,

> 'I would while it was smiling in my face
> Have plucked my nipple from his boneless gums
> And dashed the brains out' (I.7.56–8)

Lady Macbeth uses this image to persuade her husband that whatever she promised him, however extreme, she would carry out. It would be a shock to an audience that a mother could choose such a violent example; at the same time, the power of the speech conveys the strength of Lady Macbeth's convictions.

Using quotations

One of the ways in which candidates achieve high grades in an English literature examination is by the use they make of quotations. The important thing to realise is that a quotation can back up the point you wish to make.

Here are five basic points you must remember:

* Put quotation marks (inverted commas) at the beginning and end of the quotation
* Write the quotation exactly as it appears in the original
* Do not use a quotation that repeats what you have just written
* Use the quotation so that it fits into your sentence
* Keep the quotation as short as possible

Quotations should be used to develop the line of thought in your essay.

Your comment should not duplicate what is in your quotations. For example:

Lady Macbeth tells us that she wants her husband to arrive speedily so that she can pour her spirits in his ear, 'Hie thee hither / That I may pour my spirits in thine ear'.

It is far more effective to write:

Lady Macbeth tells her husband to arrive speedily so that 'I may pour my spirits in thine ear'.

Always lay out lines as they appear in the original:

> Lady Macbeth is immediately ambitious for her husband, '... and shalt be / What thou art promised'.

or:

> Lady Macbeth is immediately ambitious for her husband,
>
> '... and shalt be
> What thou art promised'.

However, the most sophisticated way of using the writer's words is to include them within your own sentence:

> The fact that Lady Macbeth may 'read strange matters' in Macbeth's face shows how well she knows his character.

Use Shakespeare's words as evidence to support your ideas. Don't just include words from the original to prove you have read it!

Literary terms

blank verse unrhymed iambic pentameter: a line of five iambs

couplet a pair of rhymed lines of any metre

doggerel bad verse – ill-constructed, rough, clumsy versification

dramatic irony when the development of the plot allows the audience to know more about what is happening than some of the characters themselves know

iambic consisting of the iamb – which is the commonest metrical foot in English verse. It has two syllables, consisting of one weak stress followed by a strong stress, ti-tum

irony saying one thing when another is meant

pentameter in versification a line of five feet – often iambic

prose any language that is not made patterned by the regularity of metre

soliloquy when a character speaks directly to the audience, as if thinking aloud